Cryptocurrency Secrets
Unlock Wealth in the Crypto World

Table of Contents

Chapter 1. Introduction

Titled "Cryptocurrency Secrets: Unlock Wealth in the Crypto World," this Special Report promises to be your beacon, illuminating your path through the often mystifying domain of digital currencies. Notably, we've made it a priority to ensure that this guide is as digestible as possible, making it suitable even for the layperson. Fret not, for we've distilled the complexity of blockchain technology into bite-size, easy-to-understand information, while still keeping you abreast with the avant-garde advancements within this dynamic field. Immerse yourself in this Special Report to unlock the often hidden treasures in the crypto world and embolden your financial empowerment. Let us demystify the technical nuances with a chirpy, engaging read that doesn't just educate, but motivates you to leverage these digital assets for wealth generation. Prepare to ride the waves of cryptocurrency, and you might just find yourself on the shores of affluence.

Chapter 2. Understanding Cryptocurrency: The Future of Finance

The journey to understanding cryptocurrency starts with recognizing the thresholds that were crossed to birth this innovative form of finance. Picture traditional financial systems as an age-old fortress, sturdy and rigid, built with regulations, stringent processes, and centralized control. Now, crypto is the new player armed with decentralization, cryptographic security, and minute to no transaction costs. Cryptocurrency promises to not only challenge this fortress but also to reshape the financial landscape completely.

2.1. A Brief History of Cryptocurrency

Cryptocurrency, an idea once brushed off as being too futuristic, has now developed into a potent catalyst for change in our world. The origin of cryptocurrency is closely related to the internet's subculture - cryptography forums and discussion groups. In late 2008, a mysterious entity named Satoshi Nakamoto published the Bitcoin Whitepaper, which served as a blueprint for how decentralization, combined with cryptographic proof, can facilitate a digital currency system without the need for a central authority. In January 2009, Nakamoto mined the genesis block, marking the beginning of Bitcoin, the first cryptocurrency.

Since Bitcoin, the world has seen the evolution of a plethora of other cryptocurrencies, also known as altcoins, each challenging the status quo with their distinct features and use-cases. As of now, there are over 4000 cryptocurrencies in circulation.

2.2. The Anatomy of Cryptocurrency

To get a comprehensive understanding of cryptocurrency, it's crucial to dissect its fundamental components:

Blockchain: Blockchain is the backbone of cryptocurrency. It is a distributed, public ledger where all confirmed transactions are included as so-called 'blocks.' It allows transparent peer-to-peer transactions to take place in a secure and auditable way.

Cryptographic Security: Cryptocurrency transactions are secured using cryptography. Every holder of a cryptocurrency has a private key, a secure digital code known only to them and their wallet. This private key proves the ownership of a public digital code, the public key, which is visible to everyone. The pair is used to authorize transactions.

Decentralization: This is the most revolutionary aspect of cryptocurrency. Unlike conventional currencies, there is no central authority that governs or regulates cryptocurrency. This means control is not universal but distributed among various participants who keep the system running.

2.3. How Cryptocurrencies Work

Cryptocurrencies operate on the premise of blockchain, cryptography, and a global consensus algorithm. Here's a simplified workflow:

1. Alice wants to send some cryptocurrency to Bob.
2. Alice signs the transaction with her private key.
3. The transaction is broadcasted to the network.
4. Network nodes validate the transaction.
5. Once validated, the transaction is added to a block.

6. The block is attached to the blockchain.

7. Bob receives the cryptocurrency from Alice.

Beyond the above process, complexities arise involving transaction fees, minting of new crypto, and the working of consensus algorithms. However, each of these revolves around the theme set by the brief workflow above.

2.4. Cryptocurrencies as a Store of Value

One of the core functions of money is to act as a store of value. In recent years, Bitcoin, in particular, has been under the spotlight, with some labeling it as 'digital gold'. The argument for Bitcoin as a store of value stems from its scarcity. Just like gold, Bitcoin has a finite supply, capped at 21 million coins. Hence, as demand swells, the price is expected to rise, thus holding value over time.

However, the volatility in cryptocurrency prices makes many skeptical about cryptocurrencies as a reliable store of value. This volatility primarily arises due to the speculative nature of the crypto market and regulatory news affecting market sentiments.

2.5. The Real-World Utility of Cryptocurrencies

Aside from being a store of value or investment tool, cryptocurrencies have numerous practical applications in the real world:

Remittances: Cryptocurrencies allow for cheap and rapid cross-border transactions, a boon for overseas workers who send money home.

Banking the Unbanked: An estimated 1.7 billion adults worldwide are unbanked, yet two-thirds of them own a mobile phone that could help them access financial services. Cryptocurrencies can break down the barriers to entry and enable financial inclusion worldwide.

Smart Contracts and DApps: The Ethereum network introduced the concept of smart contracts and Decentralized Applications (DApps), which open a world of possibilities from decentralized finance (DeFi) to games and marketplaces.

While the journey of understanding the world of cryptocurrency requires curiosity and patience, it's an undeniably rich and fascinating journey. Both a disruptive technology and a powerful financial movement, cryptocurrency is fueling talk of a financial revolution.

There are still many mysteries to unravel and potential to unfold in the realm of cryptocurrency. This is a world where technical advancement meets financial liberation, and thus, truly promises to be the future of finance, reimagined and redefined.

Chapter 3. The Birth of Bitcoin: A Deep Dive

In 2008, amidst the throes of a financial crisis that rippled across the globe, an enigmatic figure by the pseudonym of Satoshi Nakamoto presented a revolutionary solution – Bitcoin, a peer-to-peer electronic cash system. It proposed a radically new mode of financial interchange that would upend traditional banking paradigms.

3.1. The Genesis: Satoshi's White Paper

Nakamoto unveiled Bitcoin to the world through a white paper, bypassing the regular routes of academic and scientific papers. Dated October 31, 2008, "Bitcoin: A Peer-to-Peer Electronic Cash System" was shared via a cryptography mailing list. The nine-page document meticulously sketched out the proposed system's architecture and functionality, but not once did it divulge who its author was or what his motivations were.

The white paper described Bitcoin as an "electronic payment system based on cryptographic proof instead of trust, allowing any two willing parties to transact directly with each other without the need for a trusted third party." The system would have its currency - the 'bitcoin'. It was an unambiguous declaration of war on traditional finance. No more middlemen. No more banks. Freedom and control over one's wealth was in the individual's hands.

3.2. Satoshi's Disappearance and the Continuity of Bitcoin

After releasing the Bitcoin software in 2009 and working with a small community to improve and maintain it, in 2010, Nakamoto handed over control to developer Gavin Andresen and then vanished. Satoshi's anonymity and eventual disappearance didn't hinder Bitcoin. Developers continued to refine the code, while users kept mining and transacting bitcoins.

Initially, each block added to the blockchain rewarded the miner with 50 bitcoins. This 'block reward' halves approximately every four years, in an event called 'halving'. As of the time of writing, the block reward is 6.25 bitcoins.

3.3. What's Under the Hood: The Technology of Bitcoin

At its core, Bitcoin is ingenious software. It amalgamates advanced computer science principles with solid cryptographic techniques – a symbiotic, watertight, yet transparent system functioning on a decentralized network of computers. Here we deep-dive into three fundamental technologies that enable Bitcoin - the blockchain, cryptographic hash functions, and digital signatures.

The blockchain is the de facto ledger, a public, time-stamped record of all transactions. Blocks of transactions are added chronologically, forming a chain – hence the 'blockchain'. It solves the double-spending problem inherent in digital currencies by ensuring a transaction is valid based on previous transactions in the chain.

Cryptographic hash functions create a unique digital fingerprint, or 'hash', from input data of any size. Crucially, any minute change in the input data drastically alters the hash. Bitcoin employs the SHA-256 hashing algorithm, an element of its security infrastructure. Every block is hashed, and the resulting hash is included in the next block, linking them together.

Digital signatures celebrate the amalgamation of cryptography with private and public key pairs, adding an additional layer of security. They ensure the integrity and authenticity of a transaction by letting miners verify that the payor has control of the bitcoins they intend to send. The combination of these three technologies propels a cryptographic trust machine where anyone can verify transactions.

3.4. Mining: The Heartbeat of Bitcoin

In the Bitcoin ecosystem, 'mining' does two vital things: it adds blocks of transactions to the blockchain, and it brings new bitcoins into circulation. Mining is essentially solving complex mathematical problems using computational power – a process also known as 'Proof-of-Work'.

When a miner successfully mines a block, they broadcast it to the network. Other miners verify the transactions within the block and if they reach consensus, the block is added to the blockchain. The successful miner then receives the block reward and any transaction fees included by those sending transactions in the block.

3.5. Gaining Value and Acceptance

How does a system bootstrapped in the void of the internet gain value? In the early days of Bitcoin, transactions were few and trivial. In 2010, in what would go down in Bitcoin folklore, a developer named Laszlo Hanyecz bought two pizzas for 10,000 bitcoins. What is the assumed folly of Hanyecz is today valued in millions of dollars.

This event, though seemingly inconsequential, was instrumental in the Bitcoin economy - it demonstrated that bitcoin had achieved a value that was publicly agreed upon, marking the beginning of Bitcoin's acceptance as a medium of exchange.

As Bitcoin gained traction, more users joined the network, and more developers contributed to improving the software. Bitcoin's value grew as businesses started accepting it, and it was listed on cryptocurrency exchanges for trading, establishing both usability and exchangeability. Interwoven with its potential for decentralization and disruption, trust in Bitcoin rose, increasing its value.

From its cipherpunk roots to today's dynamic cryptocurrency ecosystem, Bitcoin has grown into a symbol of financial freedom and a tool for wealth creation and preservation. Satoshi's grand experiment continues to challenge conventional finance, inviting us to reconsider what money is and can be. As an investment and as a technology, Bitcoin is just beginning its journey, and whoever leverages it stands to gain from this digital rush.

Chapter 4. Ethereum and the Rise of Altcoins

In the magenta dawn of the cryptocurrency industry, Bitcoin, conceived by a mysterious entity known as Satoshi Nakamoto, was the shining star. An innovative creation, it captured everyone's imagination, riveting the world with its decentralized structure and potential for wealth generation. But though Bitcoin seized the limelight, it sparked a trend, propelling other entrepreneurs and developers to bring forward their digital brainchildren, commonly referred to as "altcoins."

Ethereum is one such altcoin that has gained groundbreaking popularity and appreciation. Its foundation is attributed to Vitalik Buterin, a Russian-Canadian prodigy, who envisaged a digital landscape where Bitcoin was not the sole player. His revolutionary idea? Ethereum - a public, open-source platform based on blockchain technology that enables developers to build and deploy decentralized applications.

4.1. Understanding Ethereum

Supporting a profound programming language, Ethereum circumvents Bitcoin's limitations, allowing developers to create a variety of applications that execute 'smart contracts.' Vitalik Buterin's vision was to create a digital environment where contractual agreements can be executed independently, without intermediaries, thus expediting transactions and increasing security.

In Ethereum's universe, 'Ether' is the cryptocurrency used to operate within this platform. It is not only a tradeable cryptocurrency but also the fuel that propowers Ethereum; Ether is used by application developers to pay for transaction fees and services on the Ethereum network.

4.2. Ethereum's Unique Selling Proposition - Smart Contracts

The concept of 'Smart Contracts,' forms the crux of Ethereum's USP, catapulting it to fame. Smart Contracts are self-executing contracts with the terms of the agreement directly written into lines of code. They permit trusted transactions without third parties, which are traceable, transparent, and irreversible.

Smart contracts make many processes more efficient. When implemented to business operations, they replace traditional contracts, minimizing the possibility of error and drastically reducing paperwork.

4.3. Ethereum vs. Bitcoin: The Tech Differentiator

Being the first to market, Bitcoin enjoys a dominant market position and brand visibility. However, Ethereum adds innovation with undeniably game-changing features. While Bitcoin introduced the concept of a decentralized, peer-to-peer digital currency, Ethereum innovates by enabling the development and execution of applications on its platform.

Additionally, while Bitcoin transactions are primarily one-dimensional, sender-to-receiver, Ethereum's transactions could contain executable code. Bitcoin's blockchain records contracts, to be sure — but Ethereum's blockchain puts a "Turing complete" programming language designed to allow developers to write more programs that enable blockchain transactions. This builds more functionality into the system.

4.4. The ICO Explosion and Ethereum

With Ethereum fundamentally shifting the way we view blockchain technology, it was only a matter of time before its potential was leveraged to raise capital. Initial Coin Offerings (ICOs) quickly gained traction - a fundraising tool where new projects sell their underlying tokens in exchange for Bitcoin, but primarily, Ethereum.

This novel fundraising method caught the attention of many and soon, ICOs began to sprout up, reshaping the traditional venture capital system. This wave culminated in 2017's ICO boom, ultimately adding to Ethereum's appeal and value.

However, while the explosion of ICOs brought prosperity, it also ushered in significant critique. From unregulated activities to outright fraudulent schemes, Ethereum's association with these activities resulted in heated debates regarding necessary legislative measures.

4.5. Ethereum 2.0: The Future Vision

Ethereum's innovativeness does not stop at smart contracts or enabling decentralized applications. With Ethereum 2.0, the platform plans to solve the most significant pain points in blockchain technology today - scalability, security, and sustainability. Ethereum 2.0 or "Serenity" will switch from Proof of Work (PoW) to Proof of Stake (PoS), which promises to optimize the platform's performance and cement its place in the future of blockchain technology.

4.6. Summation

The emergence of Ethereum brought along a legion of altcoins, each with nuanced propositions and a shared objective of expanding the capabilities of blockchain. It diversified the marketplace and exemplified the versatility of blockchain technology, extending its applications well beyond a digital currency.

Although Ethereum has its own set of challenges - such as scalability issues and competition from newly emerging platforms - its versatility, coupled with a supportive community and continuous upgrades, ensures its relevance in this hyper-evolving digital realm. Consequently, it holds immense potential for wealth generation and is a vital aspect of our crypto journey.

In essence, understanding the ever-growing altcoin landscape, particularly Ethereum, is a stepping stone to deciphering the broader complexities of the crypto world and the possibilities it holds.

Chapter 5. Inside Blockchain Technology: Databases of the Future

Blockchain technology, the backbone of cryptocurrencies, is transforming the digital landscape as it redefines what a database can be. This innovative technology isn't just about Bitcoin or Ethereum; it's setting the stage for a whole new digital world.

Let's delve into the intricate workings of blockchain technology: an unalterable, distributed ledger system safeguarding online transactions, engaging interconnected systems for veracity, and providing relentless transparency.

5.1. Understanding the Basics

Blockchain technology, as the name implies, comprises a chain of blocks. But, we're not speaking of blocks as in the traditional physical sense. In the ecosystem of blockchain, a 'block' refers to a bundle of digital information. Each block 'chains' itself to the preceding and successive blocks, hence creating the 'blockchain'.

These blocks consist of three parts: . **Data**- Defines the specifics of transactions like date, time, and the monetary amount of your most recent purchase from an online store. . **Hash**- This complex alphanumeric string individualizes the block and its data. Even minor changes to a block will modify the hash tremendously, thus aiding in the easy detection of alterations. . **Hash of the previous block**- This element effectively links one block to another and builds the chain. The presence of previous hash further reinforces security, ensuring that block data remains irreversible.

5.2. Diving Deeper: Distributed Ledger Technology

The principle at the heart of blockchain, and what sets it apart from traditional database systems, is the Distributed Ledger Technology (DLT). DLT delivers a level of security and transparency that's robust because every participant, called a node, in the vast network maintains a copy of the entire ledger. This means when a new block is added to the blockchain, every node updates their copy of the ledger. This design brings transparency to the fore, by making all transactions glaringly public.

The distributed setup makes the blockchain essentially immutable. Since the information isn't centralized, it guards against potential threats. Because no solitary organization or person has control, information can't be altered retrospectively without the consensus of the network.

5.3. Cryptography: The Purveyor of Trust

While the previous hash lends a helping hand in securing the blockchain, it alone isn't robust enough to fend off tampering attempts. To fortify security, blockchain employs a consensus mechanism in conjunction with cryptographic methods.

Participants or nodes within the blockchain use public and private keys to initiate and authenticate transactions. Public keys are like your cryptocurrency address, shared with everyone, while private keys are secret passwords that only you should know. A combination of your private key and someone else's public key creates a digital signature for secure transactions.

5.4. Consensus Mechanisms: The Heart of the Blockchain

So, how does the network collectively decide on the addition of new blocks or verify transactions? Welcome to the world of Consensus Mechanisms - the solution to the most significant challenge faced by decentralized systems. It helps to establish the version of truth within the network, preventing malicious exploitation.

Proof of Work (PoW) is a commonly used consensus mechanism in blockchains, the most notable use case being Bitcoin. In a PoW-based system, nodes or 'miners' compete against each other to solve complex mathematical problems. The one who solves it first gets to add a new block to the blockchain.

However, PoW isn't the only consensus mechanism. As blockchain technology evolves, new consensus mechanisms like Proof of Stake (PoS), Delegated Proof of Stake, and Practical Byzantine Fault Tolerance, among others, offer innovative alternatives.

5.5. Blockchain: A Digital Revolution

Despite teething trials, the potential of blockchain remains enormous. Its significance isn't solely about underpinning cryptocurrencies, but how it's transforming the business and technology spectrums. From finance and healthcare to supply chain and governance, few industries are impervious to the ground-breaking virtues of blockchain technology.

While the road to widespread acceptance is fraught with challenges, remember every groundbreaking technology must confront, and overcome, skepticism. Railroads, airplanes, the internet—all were doubted initially. But eventually, these technologies rendered themselves indispensable for the advancement of mankind.

Blockchain, with its disruptive potential, stature in ensuring transparency, and promise towards decentralization, is set to follow a similar trajectory, forging a new era in digital databases. It's not simply a technology; it's a revolution.

Chapter 6. Decoding Cryptography in Cryptocurrency

To begin our journey into the secrets of cryptocurrency, we'll venture into the heart of the matter: cryptography. Cryptography underlines the very foundation of these digital assets, ensuring security, anonymity, and integrity. Without it, the digital transactions that occur every second would be left unshielded, open to the prying eyes of malicious entities.

6.1. What is Cryptography?

Cryptography is the practice of securing communication and data in the menacing environment of the Internet. This is achieved via a collection of protocols, algorithms, and calculations. In the ordinary world, cryptography is analogous to secret messages that children send each other, where no one else knows the secret language.

The primary goal of cryptography is to ensure four things: confidentiality, integrity, non-denial, and authentication. In a nutshell: - Confidentiality: Only the intended audience can access the data. - Integrity: The data can't be altered in storage or transit without this change being detected. - Non-denial: The author can't deny the creation of data. - Authentication: The receiver can confirm the identity of the sender.

6.2. Cryptography in Cryptocurrency: An Overview

Cryptocurrency leverages cryptographic techniques to achieve decentralization, transparency, and immutability. The key cryptographic principles which give rise to the triumvirate of security, privacy, and control in the crypto sphere are: - Hashing - Digital Signature - Public Key Cryptography

6.3. Understanding Hashing

Hashing is a transformation process that takes an input (or 'message') and returns a fixed-size string of bytes. The output, called a hash, is always the same length regardless of the size of the input. It's a one-way function; that is, the data that enters the hashing function cannot be retrieved or reversed from the output.

This makes hashing a reliable method for verifying data integrity because even the smallest change in input data will cause a drastic change in the resultant hash. For instance, Bitcoin leverages the SHA-256 (Secure Hash Algorithm 256 bit) hashing function to encode transactions and verify the integrity of information.

6.4. Digital Signature

A digital signature is a mathematical scheme for demonstrating the authenticity of a digital message. Similar to the way a handwritten signature verifies the authenticity of a document, a digital signature authenticates digital documents. However, digital signatures are considerably more difficult to forge.

In the context of cryptocurrency, digital signatures ensure that cryptocoins belong to a specific user and that transactions are conducted validly. By this, it confirms that the sender has, indeed, sent the currency, and the receiver was intended.

The signing mechanism involves the application of a hash function to the message and then encrypts the result with a private key to create a signature. Identity authentication occurs when the recipient then decrypts the signature with the public key, applies the same hash function to the message, and compares the calculated hash with the decrypted hash.

6.5. Public Key Cryptography

Public Key Cryptography, also known as asymmetric cryptography, is a fundamental component of cryptocurrency infrastructure. It allows the secure, private transformation of data, even over a public network like the internet.

In this cryptographic system, a pair of keys are used: a public key for encryption and a corresponding private key for decryption. The public key is disseminated openly, while the private one is kept secret.

In the context of cryptocurrencies, the owner's public key is the address to which anyone can send bitcoins, while the private key is used to sign transactions and access funds. It's the secure combination of these keys that maintains user privacy and ensures safe transactions within the cryptocurrency network.

6.6. Cryptography: The Underlying Strength of Cryptocurrency

At its core, cryptocurrency's strength lies in the intricate weave of cryptographic principles that secure it. Hashing, digital signatures, and public key cryptography collectively ensure the integrity and security of transactions. The combination of these cryptographic techniques constructs an impregnable fortress that guards the digital wealth accumulated in your crypto-wallets against malicious threats.

Despite its complex premise, the brilliance of cryptography lies in its application. As the fuel that powers cryptocurrency, it's the invisible force enabling thousands to trade and speculate in this burgeoning financial domain. In the next chapter, we will venture further, dissecting the very anatomy of a cryptocurrency transaction.

Chapter 7. Investment Strategies for Crypto Newbies

Investing in cryptocurrencies might seem bewildering at first, especially given the volatile nature of the market. But, with a deeper look, you will realize that like any other form of investment, investing in cryptocurrencies is also based on sound principles. This section delves into the fundamental strategic aspects every crypto newbie needs to be well-versed with, making your foray into the crypto world a potentially rewarding endeavor.

7.1. Understanding the Basics

Before you set out on your investment venture, it's pivotal to equip yourself with the basic knowledge. Cryptocurrencies operate on a technology called blockchain, a decentralized technology spread across many computers that manages and records transactions. The allure of blockchain is its security.

Keep in mind, however, that the crypto market is highly volatile, with prices often exhibiting abrupt changes. This volatility can be attributed to the market's relatively small size, speculative trading, and regulatory news or events.

There are numerous cryptocurrencies available, but Bitcoin undeniably remains the largest and most recognisable. Despite its supremacy, other cryptocurrencies such as Ethereum, Binance Coin, Cardano, and many more have emerged, offering unique potential advantages and technologies.

7.2. Risk Management

Risk management is the cornerstone of any successful investment strategy. In the context of cryptocurrencies, volatility implies substantial risks, but also significant opportunities for profit. Some tips for risk management include:

- Setting Stop-Loss and Take-Profit Levels: A stop-loss level helps protect your capital against substantial losses, while a take-profit level helps ensure profitability.

- Portfolio Diversification: Invest in a variety of cryptocurrencies to spread the risk.

- Only Invest What You Can Afford to Lose: The golden rule of investment - don't invest money you can't afford to lose. This rule is particularly critical when investing in a volatile market like cryptocurrencies.

7.3. Fundamental Analysis

Fundamental analysis involves evaluating a cryptocurrency's inherent value. It necessitates a thorough understanding of the market, the coin's white paper, its use case, technology, and developer team. Questions to ask include: does the cryptocurrency solve any real-world problems? How is the project unique? Who is behind the project? Are they trustworthy and credible?

7.4. Technical Analysis

Technical Analysis involves predicting future price movements based on historical data, primarily through the use of chart patterns and technical indicators such as Moving Averages, Relative Strength Index (RSI), and others. It's incredibly useful for identifying entry and exit points for trades.

7.5. Maintaining an Investment Journal

Keeping a Journal helps track investment decisions — both good and bad. It allows you to learn from mistakes, improve strategies, and consolidate success.

7.6. Creating an Investment Portfolio

Crypto portfolio diversification involves owning several cryptocurrencies. Building a diversified portfolio begins by selecting a mix of coins that have potential but don't necessarily move upwards or downwards together. This way, some of your investments could earn profits, even while others might be losing value, effectively reducing the volatility and potential losses of your portfolio.

7.7. Staying Informed

A good crypto investor keeps themselves updated with the latest news. Regulatory announcements, technological advancements, market trends, and macroeconomic cryptocurrency data should all be on your radar.

Most importantly, remember that every investor makes bad trades occasionally. However, what separates a good investor from a poor one is their ability to learn from their mistakes. Keep refining your strategies and adjusting your approach based on new experiences and insights, and you'll find your path to success in the crypto world.

While this knowledge guide has helped demystify some of the key aspects of cryptocurrency investing, it's essential to do your own research and potentially seek advice from financial advisors to devise a strategy that suits your risk tolerance and investment goals best. Let these principles be your compass as you navigate the uncharted territories of the promising and thrilling world of cryptocurrencies.

Remember, the secret lies in leveraging calculated risks and informed decision-making. Let the crypto journey begin!

Chapter 8. Risk Management in the Crypto World

Risk management is a fundamental part of any investment strategy, and even more so in an intrinsically volatile environment like that of cryptocurrencies. Venturing into the world of digital currencies without a solid risk management plan is akin to sailing without a compass in stormy seas. Nonetheless, this chapter aims to equip you with the essential risk management strategies required for safe navigation in the paradigm-shifting currents of this new digital frontier.

8.1. Assessing Your Risk Tolerance

In the arena of cryptocurrency, understanding your personal risk tolerance is paramount. It is a measure of the amount of risk you're comfortable with taking, which is often correlated to your financial wealth, age, and investment goals. Use an investment calculator to understand how much you're willing to risk and lose without it jeopardizing your financial health.

8.2. Diversification: Spreading Your Bets

One of the cardinal tasks as part of your risk management strategy is diversification – not having all your eggs in a single basket. It involves spreading your investment across a wide range of cryptocurrencies, which not only considerably reduces the exposure to any single asset but also leverages the potential outperformance of some assets to offset underperformance by others.

8.3. Hedging Strategies

Hedging is another risk management technique used extensively across financial markets, and the cryptocurrency market is no exception. Hedging in the crypto world may involve taking opposing positions in correlated assets - such as buying a cryptocurrency and a correlated put option to protect against its price drop or investing in stablecoins that promise stability by pegging their value to an external reference, thereby providing a buffer against extreme volatility.

8.4. Understanding the Underlying Technology

Because cryptocurrencies are intrinsically linked to cutting-edge blockchain technology, understanding the fundamentals of this technology can provide insight into a coin's potential for success or failure. By understanding the problem that a digital asset solves and its corresponding unique value proposition, an investor can make informed judgments that minimize blind risk-taking.

8.5. Managing Emotional Decisions

Psychological biases can often derail even the most studied investment strategies. Awareness of these factors, such as Fear of Missing Out (FOMO) or being overly influenced by current market sentiment, can help you to mitigate their impacts.

Keeping a cool head in the face of market volatility and sticking to your investment strategy, even if it means incurring short-term losses, can make the difference between success and failure.

8.6. Importance of Robust Wallet Security

Ensuring proper security measures such as two-factor authentication (2FA), using hardware wallets for storing your coins, making regular backups of your wallets, and using secure connections for transactions are some of the fundamental ways of reducing the risk of financial loss due to security breaches.

8.7. Regular Updating and Reviewing of Your Risk Management Strategy

Your risk management strategy isn't a set-and-forget tool, but rather an evolving system that needs to be refined and adjusted continually based on market dynamics and shifts in your personal circumstances. Regular auditing and amending of your strategy will help you stay prepared for any surprises the cryptomarket conjures.

8.8. Dealing with Regulatory Risks

With governments increasingly scrutinizing cryptocurrencies and blockchain firms, understanding the regulatory landscape is vital. Keep abreast with government policies concerning digital assets to avoid legal issues that could potentially disrupt your investment.

8.9. Exit Strategy: Knowing When to Cash Out

Every good risk management plan includes an exit strategy or, at minimum, criteria that trigger consideration of an exit. Decide on an acceptable rate of return or set price targets for specific cryptocurrencies to know when to sell and cash out.

Navigating the treacherous waters of cryptocurrency investment can indeed be challenging. However, equipped with a well-planned risk management strategy and following the guidelines mentioned above, you'll find yourself better prepared to brave the storm and secure your investments from potential perils.

Chapter 9. Navigating Cryptocurrency Exchanges: A Starter Guide

In the fascinating world of cryptocurrencies, exchanges are crucial hubs where digital currencies are traded. These platforms are to cryptos what the stock exchanges are to stocks, facilitating the purchase, sale, and trade of digital assets. In this section, we'll walk you through the maze that is the world of cryptocurrency exchanges, providing you with the practical knowledge you need to navigate these platforms with confidence and safety.

9.1. Understanding Cryptocurrency Exchanges

A cryptocurrency exchange, on a fundamental level, acts as an intermediary that allows users to trade one cryptocurrency for another or for fiat currencies like USD, EUR, or INR, depending on the exchange's capabilities. Unlike traditional stock exchanges, most cryptocurrency exchanges operate 24/7, given the globally decentralized nature of the cryptocurrency market.

There are two primary types of exchanges—centralized exchanges (CEXs) and decentralized exchanges (DEXs). Centralized Exchanges like Binance, Coinbase, and Kraken are operated by a centralized entity, much like traditional banks. On the other hand, Decentralized Exchanges such as Uniswap, SushiSwap, or PancakeSwap are platforms that run on blockchain technology, permitting direct peer-to-peer transactions.

While centralized exchanges offer better liquidity, user-friendly interfaces, and customer support, they are more prone to hacking.

On the contrary, DEXs promote anonymity and remove the need for intermediaries but are often more technically complex and have issues concerning scalability and speed.

9.2. Setting Up An Account

To start trading cryptocurrencies on a platform, you'll first need to set up an account. Let's walk you through the general steps, keeping in mind that the exact process might slightly differ from exchange to exchange.

1. Visit the exchange's website and locate the 'Sign Up' or 'Register' button.

2. Enter your details, including your email address and password.

3. Complete the verification process, which usually involves confirming your email and phone number.

4. Fulfill the KYC (Know Your Customer) requirements by providing pertinent identification documents. This step enhances the security of transactions and shields against fraud.

5. Log into your newly created account, set up an additional layer of security – such as 2FA (Two-factor authentication), and proceed towards the 'deposit' section.

9.3. Funding Your Account

Before you can buy cryptocurrencies, your account needs to be funded. This can usually be done in two ways: depositing fiat currency directly or depositing a cryptocurrency like Bitcoin.

Depositing fiat currency involves linking your bank account or credit card to your exchange account and transferring funds into your exchange wallet. This step may take a day or two, depending on your bank's processing times.

On the other hand, if you choose to deposit cryptocurrency, you'll need to generate a wallet address, send the desired amount of cryptocurrency to that address, and wait for the transaction to be confirmed on the blockchain. This process is faster than a traditional bank transfer but requires you to already own cryptocurrency.

9.4. Trading Cryptocurrencies

With funds in your account, you're ready to venture into the world of cryptocurrency trading. The process differs slightly between CEXs and DEXs, but the basic principles remain the same.

In a CEX, you'll go to the trading platform and search for the trading pair you're interested in (for example, BTC/ETH). You'll then specify whether you want to 'buy' or 'sell,' the quantity you want to trade, and the price at which you want this trade to happen. Once filled, an order becomes a trade, and the corresponding cryptocurrencies will be updated in your account.

DEXs simplify this process through an Automated Market Maker model. You directly interact with a liquidity pool rather than placing an order to be matched with another user's order. This model not only ensures anonymity but saves time and reduces the complexity of matching orders.

9.5. Ensuring Security on Exchanges

Despite their convenience, cryptocurrency exchanges aren't without risks. The most notable is the risk of hacking. To protect your assets, consider implementing the following steps:

1. Use Two-Factor Authentication (2FA) for login and withdrawal requests

2. Never share any personal account information

3. Regularly update your passwords and ensure they are strong

4. Be aware of phishing attempts

5. Store your cryptocurrencies in a hardware wallet when not trading

9.6. Withdrawing Cryptocurrencies

When you're done trading, or if you've profited significantly, you may wish to withdraw your cryptos. To do this, you'll need to navigate to the withdrawal or send section of your account, specify the amount you wish to withdraw, and provide the address of the wallet you are sending to. Confirm the transaction, and the funds will be transferred to the specified wallet.

Whether you're a seasoned trader or a fresh entrant into the exciting world of cryptocurrencies, understanding how to navigate exchanges is an essential skill. With this guide, you are now equipped with the knowledge you need to grasp the dynamics of these exchanges and step into the fast-paced world of crypto trading. Remember, the key to this world is staying attentive, adapting to changes, and making informed decisions.

Chapter 10. ICO, DeFi, and NFTs: Emerging Terminologies

In the cryptocurrency domain, one might find several terminologies that are not just commonplace, but are also the pillars of this digital economy. Notably among them stand Initial Coin Offerings (ICOs), Decentralized Finance (DeFi), and Non-Fungible Tokens (NFTs), each contributing significantly to the network of transactions in the crypto universe.

ICOs, an abbreviation for Initial Coin Offerings, represent a type of funding using cryptocurrencies. They are often used by tech startups as a means to bypass the rigorous and regulated capital-raising process required by venture capitalists or banks. An ICO campaign involves selling a percentage of the cryptocurrency to early investors in exchange for legal tender or other cryptocurrencies, but mostly for Bitcoin.

10.1. Understanding ICOs

In the simplest terms, an ICO is similar to an Initial Public Offering (IPO) in the traditional economy. However, there exists a key distinction. In an IPO, investors purchase shares representing ownership in a company, whereas in an ICO, they acquire cryptocurrency tokens, often in the form of a new cryptocurrency issued by the startup.

These tokens bear similarities to company shares in that their value may increase if the company succeeds. But, they differ in that ICO tokens provide future access to a product or service, rather than a share of the company's profits. This is similar to how a Kickstarter campaign works, where backers fund a project in its early days in exchange for an early or cheaper version of the product.

To initiate an ICO, a company will generally issue a whitepaper detailing the purpose of the project, the amount of money required, and the number of tokens to be issued, along with other important details therein. Investors will then purchase these tokens using popular cryptocurrency like Bitcoin or Ethereum.

10.2. Decentralized Finance (DeFi)

As the name suggests, Decentralized Finance, or DeFi, is a financial system not governed by any central institutions, such as banks or governments. Instead, transactions are conducted on a peer-to-peer network via smart contracts on a blockchain that enforces and manages agreements without the need for a traditional financial intermediary.

The DeFi movements espouse the use of cryptocurrencies to reconstruct traditional financial systems. They encompass a broad spectrum of applications including stablecoins, lending services, crypto derivatives, insurances, prediction markets, exchanges, fund management and more.

One significant advantage of DeFi is that by eschewing centralized control, it prevents any single entity from gaining absolute control over the network. Moreover, it introduces financial inclusiveness, as anyone from any part of the world can access DeFi applications without restrictions tied to geography or capital.

10.3. Exploring DeFi

DeFi may seem overwhelming due to its wide array of complex functionalities. However, the real potential of DeFi lies in 'composability' or the ability for DeFi protocols to interact seamlessly with one another. It's often referred to as 'money legos'. You can stack different DeFi products to generate high yields or create new products.

A classic example is "yield farming" where users lend their assets to others and receive interest in return. They can then leverage these assets to borrow more assets and lend them out again to earn even more interest. This complex arrangement is possible because of how the different DeFi 'legos' interact with one another.

Remember, as promising as DeFi can be, it also comes with risks. As the sector is relatively new and unregulated, it's vulnerable to hacks and fraud. As such, it's vital to conduct due diligence before participating in the DeFi space.

10.4. Non-Fungible Tokens (NFTs)

An NFT, or Non-Funigible Token, represents assets in the digital world that are unique and therefore cannot be replaced with something else. NFTs have gained prominence in the field of digital art, where they're used to buy and sell digital artwork via blockchain technology, ensuring authenticity and ownership.

Each NFT contains distinguishing information that makes them different from each other, hence making it impossible for NFTs to be traded on a like-for-like basis. Embodied in these tokens are not just artwork, but also property rights. While anyone can view the artworks, NFTs determine who owns these pieces.

10.5. Digging Deeper into NFTs

An NFT is unique and can't be replaced with another item; they're inimitable by nature. What really brings value to an NFT is the authenticity and rarity that is established by blockchain. An oil painting for example, might have many prints, but only one original. This is the concept NFT brings to the digital world.

Popular platforms for creating and selling NFTs include OpenSea, Mintable, and Rarible. Despite the lucrative nature of NFTs, they've drawn criticism. Detractors argue that NFTs are fueling climate change since the calculations involved in the transactions require significant energy usage.

In closing, ICOs, DeFi, and NFTs are exciting terms in the cryptocurrency landscape, each serving unique functions that are reconstructing the financial and creative economy. While they brim with opportunities, it's critical to remember that they also carry a certain level of risk. However, as long as due diligence is exercised, one can partake in the evolution of this dynamic economy.

Chapter 11. Crypto Regulation and Legal Concerns: What You Need to Know

By stepping into the world of cryptocurrencies, you are entering a new frontier, one where the rules are evolving as quickly as the industry itself. Be it Bitcoin, Ethereum, or other altcoins, all of us partaking in this digital revolution must familiarize ourselves with the intricate maze of regulations and the pressing legal concerns linked to cryptocurrencies.

Starting at the beginning, cryptocurrencies came into being without much legal scrutiny. However, their meteoric rise to ubiquity attracted attention not just from investors and technologists, but from regulators worldwide. Today, crypto regulation is a subject of immense importance and quite a convoluted one at that.

11.1. Navigating the Labyrinth: Understanding Crypto Regulations

The primary challenge when it comes to legal and regulatory aspects of cryptocurrencies is their decentralized nature. Traditional financial systems and markets have central governing bodies, rules that must be obeyed, and consequences for those who don't. In contrast, decentralized networks operate peer-to-peer, with no central governing body.

Most countries, so far, have chosen to adapt their current financial regulations to incorporate cryptocurrencies. However, these efforts vary significantly across jurisdictions: while some nations embrace blockchain and its applications, others have outright banned them.

Herein lies the crux of the issue: Cryptocurrencies are global, while regulations are national. This mismatch often leads to ambiguities and loopholes that can be exploited. It's important for us as users, investors, or even enthusiasts, to understand the regulations in our own jurisdiction and, if necessary, in the jurisdiction where our exchange or wallet is based.

11.2. The Regulatory Spectrum

To comprehend how various countries are handling cryptocurrency, let's classify them into three general buckets:

1. Open regulators have embraced blockchain technology and cryptocurrencies. They recognize the innovation that blockchain brings, offering a legal framework that regulates without stifling innovation. Examples include Switzerland and Malta.

2. Cautious regulators haven't fully embraced cryptocurrencies but have not outlawed them either. They tend to apply existing financial laws to crypto assets and conduct. The United States, for example, fits this category.

3. Restrictive regulators have banned or restricted the use of cryptocurrencies significantly. They're skeptical about the promises of blockchain and are concerned about the potential risks connected to crypto, like money laundering. China is a noteworthy member of this category.

Being aware of which category your native or resident country falls in is essential in determining your legal parameters within the crypto landscape.

11.3. Crypto Regulation in the United States

In the U.S., several federal agencies claim jurisdiction over cryptocurrencies. The Securities and Exchange Commission (SEC) views most Initial Coin Offerings (ICOs) and tokens as securities, meaning they must satisfy existing securities laws. The Commodity Futures Trading Commission (CFTC) has classified Bitcoin as a commodity, while the Internal Revenue Service (IRS) treats cryptocurrencies as property, subjecting them to capital gains tax.

While this segmentation may seem confusing, understanding it can help crypto users and investors avoid legal pitfalls and tax evasion allegations. A rule of thumb is to treat your crypto assets like property or investment assets and keep records of all transactions, valuations, and income related to cryptocurrencies.

11.4. Crypto Regulation in the European Union

In the EU, regulatory focus has primarily been on Anti-Money Laundering (AML) and Counter-Terrorist Finance (CTF) concerns. The fifth Anti-Money Laundering Directive (5AMLD) came into effect in 2020 and brought many crypto service providers under the umbrella of regulated entities for the first time.

EU Member States are obligated to incorporate these requirements into their legislation. Therefore, cryptocurrency exchanges and wallet providers must now follow the same rules as traditional financial institutions regarding customer diligence and reporting suspicious transactions.

11.5. Legal Challenges and Concerns

With the evolving regulatory status of cryptocurrencies, a number of legal challenges have arisen. These predominantly revolve around consumer protection, tax evasion, AML controls, and the use of crypto in illicit activities.

Countries that are cautious or restrictive typically cite consumer protection as their primary concern. ICOs have been associated with scams, and even honest projects can fail, leading to a total loss of investment for consumers.

Crypto's pseudonymous nature makes it appealing for tax evasion. As mentioned earlier, many countries treat crypto as property, which can create confusing tax implications, especially when crypto-assets are treated differently by various tax jurisdictions.

AML and CTF regulations pose another legal challenge. Crypto exchanges have been required to incorporate stricter verification procedures, much like traditional financial institutions, to adhere to these laws. However, decentralized and peer-to-peer platforms provide ways to avoid such controls.

Finally, the use of cryptocurrencies in unlawful activities poses a significant concern due to the semi-anonymous nature of most digital currencies, which could make it harder for law enforcement agencies to trace transactions.

11.6. The Way Forward

The regulatory landscape for cryptocurrencies is still a work in progress, but strides are being made. More nations are crafting regulations tailored specifically to cryptocurrencies, and major players in the financial world, such as banks and investment firms, are putting their weight behind digital assets.

On the downside, these changes could mean more rules and restrictions, forcing crypto users, businesses, and innovators to navigate a growing array of regulatory decisions. But on the upside, it also grants more legitimacy and stability to the industry, attracting institutional investors and adoption by major businesses.

In the future, expect the legal and regulatory scenario to change even more dramatically as governments, regulators, and the crypto community define a shared path for the progress of this remarkable technology.

In conclusion, understanding the legalities, regulations, and risks associated with cryptocurrencies is critical to safely and effectively engage with them. Whether we're casual users, active traders, or blockchain early adopters, adherence to this emerging framework will contribute significantly towards the landscape of a regulated and safer cryptocurrency realm.

Remember: with great power comes great responsibility. When used responsibly, cryptocurrencies hold great potential for wealth creation and financial freedom. It's in our hands to ensure we use it within the legal and ethical frameworks of our respective jurisdictions.

www.ingramcontent.com/pod-product-compliance
Lightning Source LLC
Chambersburg PA
CBHW062304290526
45794CB00006B/2688

* 9 7 9 8 8 5 4 8 9 7 1 7 4 *